MASOOR DAL
(SPLIT RED LENTILS)

YELLOW MOONG DAL
(SPLIT YELLOW GRAM)

URAD DAL
(SPLIT BLACK LENTILS),
WITH SKIN

D1028296

MALPAUS WITH SHAHI RABADI

DALS

TARLA DALAL
India's #1 Cookery Author

S&C
SANJAY & CO.
MUMBAI

Third Printing : 2005

Copyright © Sanjay & Co.

ISBN : 81-86469-92-3

Price: Rs.89/-

Published & Distributed by : **Sanjay & Company**

353/A-1, Shah & Nahar Industrial Estate, Dhanraj Mill Compound,
Lower Parel (W), Mumbai - 400 013. INDIA.
Tel. : (91-22) 2496 8068 ● Fax : (91-22) 2496 5876 ● E-mail : sanjay@tarladalal.com

Printed by : **Jupiter Prints**, Mumbai

Recipe Research & Production Design	**Nutritionist**	**Photography**	**Design**
Pinky Chandan Dixit	Nisha Katira	Jignesh Jhaveri	Satyamangal Rege
Arati Fedane	**Food Stylist**	**Typesetting**	
Pradnya Sundararaj	Shubhangi Dhaimade	Adityas Enterprises	

BULK PURCHASES

Tarla Dalal Cookbooks are ideal gifts. If you are interested in buying more than 500 assorted copies of Tarla Dalal Cookbooks at special prices, please contact us at 91-22-2496 8068 or
email : sanjay@tarladalal.com

∼ INTRODUCTION ∼

Dal has a special place on dinning tables across India, so much so that no traditional Indian meal would seem complete without it. From humble beginnings of just a pot of pulses simmering on firewood, dal has evolved into a variety of forms as diverse in taste as the mild Maharashtrian varan to the tongue tickling sambar from the south.

Though every region boasts dals of their own special flavor, what delights me is that the simplest and most basic ingredients yield exotic recepies. Not only that but it is also a storehouse of protein and rich in calcium, iron and B vitamins.

The recipes in this book have been adapted to suit today's fast paced lifestyle and a variety of palates. Ghee and oil quantities have been limited while retaining the traditional taste.

I have divided my book into 3 sections:

Everyday dals which consists of recipes like Kairi Dal, Methiche Varan, Kerala Style Tomato Dal etc.

Celebration Dals like Dal Makhani, Panchamel Dal, Tittori and many more.. which are a must have for special occasions

Dals that Make up a Meal like Dal Dhokli, Dhanshaak Dal etc.

So, pull out your apron, roll up your sleeves and surprise your family and friends with an amazing variety of dals that will turn each meal into a gastronomic adventure. The aromatic flavor of dals will never fail to spice up your evenings in the kitchen and on the dinning table too.

Tarla Dalal

～ CONTENTS ～

EVERYDAY DALS

Hariyali Dal 9

Gujarati Dal 11

Chana Dal With Cucumber 14

Green Dal Fry 16

Mixed Dal 18

Whole Masoor Dal 21

Sambar 23

Palak Toovar Dal 26

Masala Dal 28

Masoor Dal With Spinach 30

Suva Moong Dal 32

Trevati Dal 33

Mooli Moong Dal 35

Hare Lasun ki Dal 38

Khatta Moong 40

Methiche Varan 42

Turai Aur Moong Ki Dal 44

Kerala Style Tomato Dal 46

CELEBRATION DALS

Dal Tadka 49

Dal Banjari 51

Panchratni Dal 53

Dal Makhani 56

Tittori (Parsi Dal) 58

Dal Moghlai 60

Panchmel Dal 62

Dhabey Ki Dal 64

Khandeshi Dal 67

Shajahani Dal 70

Spicy Sindhi Dal 72

Rangoon No Vaal 74

Kottu (Sri Lankan Dal) 77

DALS THAT MAKE A MEAL

Dakho (Khatti Mithi Dal With
Vegetables) 80

One Dish Dal 82

Dal Pinni 84

Chana Ghassi 87

Panchras Dal 88

Dal Dhokli 91

Dhansaak Dal 95

Darbari Dal 98

Rajma Saagwala 100

BASIC RECIPE

Coconut Milk 102

Everyday Dals

～ Hariyali Dal ～

1 cup masoor dal (split red lentils)
1 cup chopped spinach (palak) leaves
1 cup chopped fenugreek (methi) leaves
½ cup chopped coriander
½ cup chopped onions
1 tsp cumin seeds (jeera)
2 tsp amchur (dry mango powder)
½ cup chopped tomatoes
½ tsp turmeric powder (haldi)
¾ tsp chilli powder
3 tbsp ghee
salt to taste

To be ground into a paste
6 cloves garlic
6 green chillies
25 mm. (1") piece ginger

1. Clean, wash and soak the masoor dal in water for about 30 minutes. Drain.
2. Add the turmeric powder, salt and 2 cups of water and pressure cook till the dal is done.
3. Whisk well to mash the dal. Keep aside.
4. Heat the ghee in a large pan, add the onions and cumin seeds and fry for at least 2 minutes.
5. Add the spinach, fenugreek leaves, coriander, amchur powder, tomatoes, turmeric powder, chilli powder, ground paste and salt and sauté for a couple of minutes.
6. Add the cooked dal and ½ cup of water and bring to a boil.
7. Simmer for a few minutes on a low flame and serve hot.

∼ Gujarati Dal ∼

•• Preparation time : 10 minutes. •• Cooking time : 60 minutes. •• Serves 8 to10.

2 cups toovar (arhar) dal
1 cup chopped yam (suran)
2 tbsp peanuts
2 dry dates (kharekh), optional
salt to taste

For the tempering
¼ tsp mustard seeds (rai)
¼ tsp cumin seeds (jeera)
¼ tsp fenugreek (methi) seeds
10 to 12 curry leaves
2 cloves (laung)
2 sticks cinnamon (dalchini)
1 bay leaf (tejpatta)
2 small round dry red chillies
½ tsp asafoetida (hing)

2 tbsp ghee
1 tbsp oil

Other ingredients
8 pieces cocum, soaked
½ cup chopped tomatoes
2 tbsp jaggery (gur)
juice of ½ lemon
1 piece ginger, diced
4 green chillies, slit
½ tsp chilli powder
½ tsp turmeric powder (haldi)

For the garnish
4 tbsp chopped coriander

1. Clean, wash and pressure cook the dal in 4 cups of water.
2. In another vessel, cook the yam, peanuts and dry dates in a little water.
3. When the dal is cooked, cool slightly and whisk so it is smooth.
4. Prepare the tempering by heating the ghee and oil and adding the mustard seeds, cumin seeds, fenugreek seeds, curry leaves, cloves, cinnamon, bay leaf, red chillies

and asafoetida.

5. Add 3 cups of water, cocum, tomatoes, jaggery, lemon juice, ginger, green chillies, chilli powder and turmeric powder and simmer for 10 minutes.

6. Add the dal, yam pieces, peanuts, dry dates and salt and simmer for 10 to 15 minutes.

   Serve hot garnished with the chopped coriander.

Handy tips : 1. The longer this dal is simmered, the better it tastes.
2. Cocum imparts sourness to any dish. It is used in Gujarati and Maharashtrian cuisines. If you do not have kokum, use tamarind instead.

∽ Chana Dal With Cucumber ∽

∾ Preparation time : 10 minutes. ∾ Cooking time : 20 minutes. ∾ Serves 4.

¾ cup chana dal (split Bengal gram)
½ cup finely chopped cucumber
1 tsp cumin seeds (jeera)
1 tsp ginger-green chilli paste
a pinch turmeric powder (haldi)
½ tsp chilli powder
1 tsp oil
salt to taste

For the garnish
1 tbsp chopped coriander

1. Wash and soak the chana dal in water for at least an hour. Drain and keep aside.
2. Add 2 cups water to the soaked dal and pressure cook for 10 to 15 minutes, till the dal is done.
3. Whisk well to mash the dal. Keep aside.

4. Heat the oil in a large pan, add the cumin seeds and allow them to crackle.
5. Add the cooked dal, ginger-green chilli paste, turmeric powder and chilli powder and cook for 2 to 3 minutes.
6. Add the cucumber and salt and simmer for 10 to 15 minutes till the cucumber is tender, but still a little crisp. Add some water, if required to adjust the consistency. Garnish with the chopped coriander and serve hot with rice or rotis.

~ Green Dal Fry ~

•• Preparation time : 10 minutes. •• Cooking time : 25 minutes. •• Serves 4 to 6.

½ cup toovar (arhar) dal
½ cup yellow moong dal (split yellow gram)
¼ tsp turmeric powder (haldi)
2 tbsp oil
salt to taste

For the green paste
1 cup chopped coriander
½ cup freshly grated coconut
½ cup sliced onions
12 mm. (½″) piece ginger
4 green chillies
4 cloves garlic
1 tsp lemon juice

For the green paste
Combine all the ingredients required and grind to a coarse paste adding a little water if required.

How to proceed
1. Clean, wash and soak the dals in water for about 30 minutes. Drain.
2. Add the salt, turmeric powder and 3 cups of water and pressure cook till the dals are done.
3. Whisk well to mash the dals.
4. Heat oil in a large pan, add the green paste and sauté for 2 to 3 minutes.
5. Add the cooked dal and ½ cup of water and bring to a boil.
   Serve hot.

~ Mixed Dal ~

Picture on facing page

•→ Preparation time : 10 minutes. •→ Cooking time : 40 minutes. •→ Serves 4 to 6.

1 tbsp yellow moong dal (split yellow gram)
1 tbsp masoor dal (split red lentils)
1 tbsp urad dal (split black lentils)
1 tbsp chana dal (split Bengal gram)
2 tbsp toovar (arhar) dal
1 tsp cumin seeds (jeera)
½ cup chopped onions
2 tsp coriander (dhania) powder
1 tsp chilli powder
½ tsp turmeric powder (haldi)
3 tbsp ghee
salt to taste

For the tempering
½ cup chopped tomatoes
1 cup fresh curds (dahi)

MIXED DAL : Recipe above →

½ tsp garam masala
2 tbsp butter

For the garnish
chopped coriander

1. Wash all the dals. Soak in water for 30 minutes. Drain.
2. Heat the ghee in a pan and add the cumin seeds.
3. When the seeds crackle add the onions and sauté till they turn translucent.
4. Add all the dals and stir for 4 to 5 minutes.
5. Add 4 cups of water and cook on a slow flame until soft.
6. Add the coriander powder, chilli powder, turmeric powder and salt. Cover and simmer on a low flame until $2/3^{rds}$ of the water has been evaporated.
7. Whisk well to mash the dals.
8. Prepare the tempering by melting the butter in a small pan, adding the tomatoes, curds and garam masala and cooking on a slow flame for 1 to 2 minutes.
9. Add to the cooked dals and simmer for 3 to 4 minutes till it comes to a boil. Garnish with the chopped coriander and serve hot.

∽ Whole Masoor Dal ∽

↦ Preparation time : 10 minutes. ↦ Cooking time : 40 minutes. ↦ Serves 6.

1 cup whole masoor (whole red lentils)
1 cup sliced onions
¾ cup chopped tomatoes
7 to 8 small whole onions
4 tbsp ghee
salt to taste

To be ground into a paste
8 cloves garlic
8 whole dry red chillies
2 tsp coriander (dhania) seeds
1 tsp cumin seeds (jeera)
35 mm. (1½") piece ginger

For the garnish
chopped coriander

1. Wash the masoor, add 2½ cups of water and the whole onions and cook in a pressure cooker till the masoor is soft.
2. Heat the ghee in a large pan and fry the onions till they turn transluscent.
3. Add the ground paste and fry for 3 to 4 minutes.
4. Add the cooked masoor, 1 cup of water and salt and simmer for 5 minutes.
5. Add the tomatoes and simmer for another 10 minutes.
   Serve hot, garnished with the chopped coriander.

~ Sambar ~

↦ Preparation time : 15 minutes. ↦ Cooking time : 30 minutes. ↦ Serves 6 to 8.

1 cup toovar (arhar) dal
1 cup white pumpkin (lauki), cut into 1 ' pieces
6 to 8 pieces drumsticks (optional)
1 teaspoon mustard seeds (rai)
1 teaspoon fenugreek (methi) seeds
6 to 7 curry leaves
2 pinches asafoetida (hing)
2 tablespoons sambar powder (recipe below)
7 small Madras onions
2 tablespoons tamarind (imli)
1 tablespoon chopped coriander
1 large or 2 medium tomatoes, quartered
2 tablespoons oil
salt to taste

For the sambar powder
3 to 4 whole dry red chillies
2 tsp coriander (dhania) seeds
½ tsp fenugreek (methi) seeds
2 tsp toovar (arhar) dal
2 tsp chana dal (split Bengal gram)
2 tsp urad dal (split black gram)
½ tsp turmeric powder (haldi)
¼ tsp asafoetida (hing)
1 tsp oil

For sambar powder
1. Heat the oil and roast all the ingredients for the sambar masala in it.
2. Grind to a fine powder in a blender. Keep aside and use as required.

How to proceed
1. Clean and wash the dal. Soak in water for about 30 mins. Drain.
2. Add 3 cups of water and pressure cook the dal until soft.
3. Whisk well to mash the dal. Keep aside.
4. Meanwhile boil the pumpkin with the drumsticks in 1½ cups of water. Drain and add to the dal. If you like, boil the onions with the pumpkin.

5. Soak the tamarind in a little water and keep aside for 30 minutes. Rub the tamarind by hand and strain. Add to the dal mixture.
6. Heat the oil in a small pan and fry the mustard seeds and fenugreek seeds.
7. When the seeds crackle, add the curry leaves and fry for 2 to 3 minutes.
8. Add the asafoetida, cooked dal mixture, sambhar powder, chopped coriander and salt and boil for 5 to 7 minutes.
9. Add the tomatoes and boil again for 2 to 3 minutes.
   Serve hot.

~ Palak Toovar Dal ~

•• Preparation time : 20 minutes. •• Cooking time : 20 minutes. •• Serves 3.

½ cup toovar (arhar) dal
2 cups chopped spinach (palak)
1 tsp finely chopped ginger
1 tsp finely chopped green chillies
¼ tsp turmeric powder (haldi)
1 tsp lemon juice
½ tsp chilli powder
2 tbsp chopped coriander
salt to taste

For the tempering
3 bay leaves (tejpatta)
3 cloves (laung)
3 whole dry red chillies, broken into pieces
½ tsp cumin seeds (jeera)
a pinch asafoetida (hing)

2 tbsp oil

1. Clean, wash and soak the toovar dal in water for 2 hours. Drain and keep aside.
2. Combine the soaked toovar dal, ginger, green chillies, turmeric powder, salt and 3 cups of water and pressure cook for 2 whistles.
3. Transfer to a large pan, add the spinach and lemon juice and bring to a boil.
4. For the tempering, heat the oil in a pan. Add the bay leaves, cloves, red chillies, cumin seeds and asafoetida.
5. When the seeds crackle, pour the tempering over the cooked dal. Add the chilli powder and chopped coriander, mix well and simmer for 4 to 5 minutes.
   Serve hot.

~ Masala Dal ~

↔ Preparation time : 20 minutes. ↔ Cooking time : 30 minutes. ↔ Serves 4 to 6.

¼ cup yellow moong dal (split yellow gram)
¼ cup masoor dal (split red lentil)
¼ cup urad dal (split black grams)
½ cup toovar (arhar) dal
¾ cup grated onions
¾ cup chopped tomatoes
3 tbsp oil
salt to taste

To be ground into a paste
5 cloves garlic
2 tsp coriander (dhania) seeds
1 tsp cumin seeds (jeera)
¼ tsp turmeric powder (haldi)
1 tbsp chopped coriander
6 Kashmiri dry red chillies

25 mm. (1″) piece ginger
3 sticks cinnamon (dalchini)
3 peppercorns
3 cloves (laung)

For the garnish
chopped coriander

1. Wash all the dals together and soak in water for 30 minutes. Drain.
2. Add 3 cups of water and cook until done in a pressure cooker.
3. Heat the oil and fry the onions till they turn translucent.
4. Add the ground paste and fry for 3 to 4 minutes.
5. Add the tomatoes and fry again for 3 to 4 minutes.
6. Add the cooked dals ½ cup of water and salt.
7. Bring to a boil and simmer for 5 to 7 minutes. Garnish with the chopped coriander and serve hot.

~ Masoor Dal With Spinach ~

↔ Preparation time : 10 minutes. ↔ Cooking time : 20 minutes. ↔ Serves 4.

¾ cup masoor dal (split red lentils)
1 cup chopped spinach (palak)
1 tsp ginger-green chilli paste
a pinch turmeric powder (haldi)
3 green cardamoms (elaichi)
1 tsp cumin seeds (jeera)
3 whole dry red chillies, broken into pieces
6 to 8 curry leaves
1 tsp chopped garlic
1 tbsp tamarind (imli) pulp
1 tsp oil
salt to taste

1. Clean, wash and soak the masoor dal in water for about 30 minutes. Drain.
2. Add the ginger-green chilli paste and turmeric powder to the dal along with 2 cups of water and pressure cook for 10 to 15 minutes, until the dal is cooked.

3. Whisk well to mash the dal. Keep aside.
4. Heat the oil in a pan, add the cardamoms and cumin seeds.
5. When the cumin seeds crackle, add the dry red chillies, curry leaves and garlic and sauté for 1 minute.
6. Add the dal, tamarind pulp, spinach and salt and ½ cup of water and bring to a boil.
7. Simmer for a few minutes and serve hot.

∽ Suva Moong Dal ∽

↦ Preparation time : 10 minutes. ↦ Cooking time : 25 minutes. ↦ Serves 4 to 6.

1 cup yellow moong dal (split yellow gram)
¼ tsp turmeric powder (haldi)
½ tsp cumin seeds (jeera)
2 to 3 curry leaves
2 tsps chopped garlic
½ tsp chopped green chilli
½ cup finely chopped onions
2 tbsp chopped dill (shepu bhaji/suva bhaji) leaves
2 tbsp oil
salt to taste

1. Clean, wash and soak the dal in water for about 30 minutes. Drain.
2. Add the turmeric powder, salt and 3 cups of water and pressure cook till the dal is done. Whisk well to mash the dal and keep aside.
3. Heat oil in a large pan and add the cumin seeds. When the seeds crackle, add the curry leaves, garlic, green chilli, onions and sauté till the onions turn translucent.
4. Add the cooked dal, dill leaves, 1 cup of water and bring to a boil. Simmer for 10 minutes and serve hot.

32

~ Trevati Dal ~

↠ Preparation time : 15 minutes. ↠ Cooking time : 30 minutes. ↠ Serves 6 to 8.

½ cup chana dal (split Bengal gram)
½ cup toovar (arhar) dal
½ cup green moong dal (split green gram)
1 tsp cumin seeds (jeera)
2 cloves (laung)
1 bay leaf (tejpatta)
2 whole dried red chillies
½ tsp asafoetida (hing)
½ cup finely chopped onions
1 to 2 green chillies, chopped
2 tbsp finely chopped garlic
1 tsp chopped ginger
½ cup chopped tomatoes
1 tsp chilli powder
½ tsp turmeric powder (haldi)
juice of 1 lemon

2 to 3 tbsp oil
salt to taste

For the garnish
chopped coriander

1. Clean, wash and soak the dals in water about 30 minutes. Drain.
2. Pressure cook the dals in 3 cups of water. Keep aside.
3. Heat the oil in a pan, add the cumin seeds, cloves, bay leaf, red chillies and asafoetida and fry for a few seconds.
4. Add the onions, green chillies, garlic and ginger and fry for a few more minutes.
5. Add the tomatoes, chilli powder and turmeric powder and stir well, till the oil separates from the masala.
6. Add the dals and 2 cups of water.
7. Add the lemon juice and salt and simmer for 10 minutes.
Serve hot garnished with the chopped coriander.

Handy tip : To make a "Jain" Trevati Dal, omit the onions, ginger and garlic and proceed as per the recipe.

~ Mooli Moong Dal ~

Picture on page 37

•• Preparation time : 15 minutes. •• Cooking time : 20 minutes. •• Serves 3.

½ cup yellow moong dal (split yellow gram)
1 cup finely chopped white radish (mooli)
½ tsp turmeric powder (haldi)
½ tsp cumin seeds (jeera)
1 bay leaf (tejpatta)
2 cloves (laung)
2 tsp finely chopped green chillies
½ tsp grated ginger
¼ tsp asafoetida (hing)
1 tsp chilli powder
½ cup chopped coriander
1 tbsp ghee
salt to taste

1. Soak the moong dal in water for about 30 minutes. Drain.
2. Combine the dal, radish, turmeric powder and salt with 2 cups of water and

pressure cook till the dal is tender.

3. Whisk well to mash the dal. Keep aside.
4. Heat the ghee in a large pan and add the cumin seeds, bay leaf and cloves.
5. When the seeds crackle, add the green chillies, ginger, asafoetida and chilli powder and mix well.
6. Add the cooked dal and ½ cup of water and simmer for 4 to 5 minutes.
7. Add the chopped coriander and mix well.
   Serve hot.

MOOLI MOONG DAL : Recipe on page 35 ➜

～ Hare Lasun Ki Dal ～

→ Preparation time : 10 minutes. → Cooking time : 25 minutes. → Serves 4 to 6.

1 cup toovar (arhar) dal
¼ tsp turmeric powder (haldi)
½ cup finely chopped green garlic (lasun)
½ tsp cumin seeds (jeera)
2 whole dry red chillies, broken into pieces
½ tsp ginger-garlic paste
¼ tsp asafoetida (hing)
¼ cup chopped tomatoes
2 tbsp oil
salt to taste

For the garnish
chopped coriander

1. Clean, wash and soak the dal in water for about 30 minutes. Drain.
2. Add the turmeric powder, salt and 3 cups of water and pressure cook till the dal is

done.
3. Whisk well and keep aside.
4. Heat the oil in a pan and add the cumin seeds.
5. When the seeds crackle, add the dry red chillies, ginger-green chilli paste, asafoetida and green garlic and sauté for 2 to 3 minutes.
6. Add the tomatoes and sauté till the mixture leaves oil
7. Add the cooked dal and ½ cup of water and bring to a boil.
   Serve hot garnished with the chopped coriander.

Handy tip : A mixture of chopped coriander and garlic can be substituted when green garlic is not in season.

～ Khatta Moong ～

•→ Preparation time : 20 minutes. •→ Cooking time : 20 minutes. •→ Serves 4 to 6.

1 cup whole moong (whole green gram)
1 cup sour curds (dahi)
½ tsp chilli powder
½ tsp turmeric powder (haldi)
1 tsp mustard seeds (rai)
3 to 4 curry leaves
¼ tsp asafoetida (hing)
1 tsp green chilli-ginger paste
2 tbsp oil
salt to taste

1. Wash the moong and pressure cook it in 1½ cups of water for 2 whistles. The dal should be cooked but not mashed.
2. Beat the curds with the chilli powder and turmeric powder.
3. Heat the oil in a pan, add the mustard seeds, curry leaves and asafoetida and stir.
4. Add the moong and mix gently.

5. Add the beaten curds, green chilli-ginger paste and salt and mix well.
6. Simmer for 10 to 15 minutes.
   Serve hot with plain rice.

Handy tip : If the curds are fresh, add ½ tsp of citric acid.

~ Methiche Varan ~

Picture on back cover

•• Preparation time : 10 minutes. •• Cooking time : 25 minutes. •• Serves 4.

1 cup finely chopped fenugreek (methi) leaves
1 cup toovar (arhar) dal
1 tsp jaggery (gur), optional
¼ tsp turmeric powder (haldi)
½ tsp chilli powder
salt to taste

For the tempering
¼ tsp asafoetida (hing)
4 to 5 clover garlic, crushed (optional)
2 tbsp ghee / oil

1. Clean, wash and soak the dal in water for about 30 minutes. Drain.
2. Pressure cook the dal with turmeric powder, salt and 3 cups of water till the dal is done.
3. Whisk well, add ½ cup of water, jaggery and chilli powder and bring to a boil.

42

4. Meanwhile, heat the ghee in a small pan and add the asafoetida and garlic.
5. Sauté till the garlic turns golden brown.
6. Add the fenugreek leaves and sauté for 2 minutes.
7. Pour this tempering over the cooked dal and mix well.
   Serve hot.

~ Turai Aur Moong Ki Dal ~

↪ Preparation time : 15 minutes. ↪ Cooking time : 30 minutes. ↪ Serves 4 to 6.

1 cup yellow moong dal (split yellow gram)
4 cups turai (ridge gourd), peeled and chopped
1 tsp ginger-green chilli paste
¼ tsp turmeric powder (haldi)
1 cup finely chopped onions
1 tsp cumin seeds (jeera)
a pinch asafoetida (hing)
1 tsp chilli powder
1 tsp garam masala
1 tbsp oil
salt to taste

For the garnish
¼ cup chopped coriander

1. Clean, wash and soak the moong dal in water for about 30 minutes. Drain.

2. Combine the moong dal, ginger-green chilli paste, turmeric powder and salt with 3 cups of water and pressure cook for 2 to 3 whistles or until the dal is cooked.
3. Whisk well to mash the dal. Keep aside.
4. Meanwhile heat the oil in a large pan and add the onions to it. Sauté for a few minutes till the onions turn translucent and then add the turai, salt and about ½ cup of water.
5. Cover and cook on a medium flame till the turai is done.
6. Add the cooked dal and ½ cup of water, if required, and bring to a boil. Keep aside.
7. For the tempering, heat the oil in a small pan, add the cumin seeds, asafoetida, chilli powder and garam masala and fry till the seeds crackle.
8. Pour this tempering over the prepared dal.
   Serve hot, garnished with the coriander.

～ Karela Style Tomato Dal ～

•• Preparation time : 10 minutes. •• Cooking time : 35 minutes. •• Serves 4.

1 cup toovar (arhar) dal
2 green chillies, slit lengthwise
½ cup chopped tomatoes
1 tbsp grated jaggery (gur)
¼ tsp turmeric powder (haldi)
salt to taste

To be ground into a smooth paste
¼ cup freshly grated coconut
1 whole dry red chilli, broken into pieces
½ tsp cumin seeds (jeera)
¼ cup water

For the tempering
½ tsp mustard seeds (rai)
1 whole dry red chilli, broken into pieces

46

4 to 5 curry leaves
¼ cup chopped onions
2 tbsp oil

1. Clean, wash and soak the dal in water for about 30 minutes. Drain.
2. Pressure cook the dal with turmeric powder, salt and 3 cups of water till soft.
3. Whisk well, add the green chillies, tomatoes, jaggary, coconut paste and 1 cup of water. Bring to boil and simmer for 10 minutes.
4. To make the tempering, heat oil in a small pan and add the mustard seeds.
5. When the seeds crackle, add the dry red chilli and curry leaves.
6. Add the chopped onions and sauté till the onions turn golden brown in colour.
7. Pour over the dal and mix well.
   Serve hot.

Celebration
Dals

Dal Tadka

Picture on cover

Preparation time : 10 minutes. Cooking time : 25 minutes. Serves 6.

1 cup red masoor dal (split red lentils)
¼ cup yellow moong dal (split yellow gram)
2 green chillies, slit
1 tsp grated ginger
1 tsp grated garlic
¼ tsp turmeric powder (haldi)
salt to taste

For the tempering
½ tsp mustard seeds (rai)
½ tsp nigella seeds (kalonji)
1 whole dry red chilli
½ cup sliced onions
½ cup chopped tomatoes
2 tbsp ghee

For the garnish
3 tbsp chopped coriander
1 tbsp butter

1. Wash the dals together.
2. Combine the dals, green chillies, ginger, garlic, turmeric powder, salt and 3 cups of water and pressure cook till the dals are tender.
3. Remove the chillies and discard. Whisk the dal till it is smooth. Keep aside.

For the tempering
1. Heat the ghee in a pan and add the mustard seeds, nigella seeds and red chilli.
2. When the mustard seeds crackle, add the onions and sauté till they are translucent.
3. Add the tomatoes and sauté for another 3 to 4 minutes.

How to proceed
Add the dals to the tempering, mix well and bring to a boil.
Serve hot, garnished with the coriander and butter.

~ Dal Banjari ~

↔ Preparation time : 15 minutes. ↔ Cooking time : 30 minutes. ↔ Serves 6.

1 cup urad dal (split black lentils with skin)
½ cup chana dal (split Bengal gram)
¼ tsp turmeric powder (haldi)
½ cup sliced onions
2 cloves (laung)
1 stick cinnamon (dalchini)
2 dry whole red chillies, broken into pieces
2 tsp ginger-garlic paste
1 tsp finely chopped green chillies
1 tsp chilli powder
2 tbsp ghee
salt to taste

For the garnish
chopped coriander
ginger, cut into thin strips (juliennes)

1. Clean and wash the dals together. Pressure cook with the turmeric powder, salt and 3 cups of water for 4 to 5 whistles or until the dal is cooked.
2. Heat the ghee in a pan, add the onions, cloves, cinnamon and red chillies and sauté till onions turn golden brown.
3. Add the ginger-garlic paste, green chillies and chilli powder and sauté for 2 minutes.
4. Add this to the cooked dal and boil for 4 to 5 minutes.
   Serve hot garnished with the chopped coriander and ginger strips.

~ Panchratni Dal ~

Picture on page 55

↔ Preparation time : 15 minutes. ↔ Cooking time : 25 minutes. ↔ Serves 6 to 8.

¼ cup whole moong (whole green gram)
¼ cup whole masoor (whole red lentils)
¼ cup whole urad (whole black lentils)
¼ cup chana dal (split Bengal gram)
¼ cup toovar (arhar) dal
3 cardamoms (elaichi)
25 mm. (1") stick cinnamon (dalchini)
1 tsp cumin seeds (jeera)
½ cup chopped onions
¼ cup chopped tomatoes
1 tsp coriander (dhania) powder
2 tsp chilli powder
¼ tsp turmeric powder (haldi)
½ tsp cumin (jeera) powder
1½ tsp fennel (saunf) powder
½ cup curds (dahi), whisked

2 tsp oil
salt to taste

For the garnish
2 tbsp chopped coriander

1. Clean, wash and soak the dals in warm water for at least an hour. Drain and keep aside.
2. Add 4 cups water and cook in a pressure cooker for 15 to 20 minutes, over medium flame, till the dals are cooked.
3. Heat the oil in a pan, add the cardamoms, cinnamon and cumin seeds and allow the cumin seeds to crackle.
3. Add the onions and cook till they are golden brown.
4. Add the tomatoes, coriander powder, red chilli powder, turmeric powder, cumin powder and fennel powder and cook for 4 to 5 minutes.
5. Add the curds and cook for 2 to 3 minutes.
6. Add the cooked dals and salt and allow the dal to come to a boil.
   Garnish with coriander and serve hot with rice or rotis.

PANCHRATNI DAL : Recipe on page 53 →

~ Dal Makhani ~

↠ Preparation time : 15 minutes. ↠ Cooking time : 20 to 25 minutes. ↠ Serves 4 to 6.

¾ cup whole urad (whole black lentils)
2 tbsp rajma (kidney beans)
1 tsp cumin seeds (jeera)
2 green chilles, slit
25 mm. (1") stick cinnamon (dalchini)
2 cloves (laung)
3 cardamoms (elaichi)
½ cup finely chopped onions
½ tsp ginger-garlic paste
1 tsp chilli powder
¼ tsp turmeric powder (haldi)
1½ cups fresh tomato pulp
¾ cup (150 grams) cream
3 tbsp butter
salt to taste

For the garnish
2 tbsp chopped coriander
1 tbsp butter

1. Clean, wash and soak the whole urad and rajma overnight. Drain and keep aside.
2. Combine the dals and salt with 2 cups of water and pressure cook till the dals are overcooked. Whisk well till the dal is almost mashed.
3. Heat the butter in a pan and add the cumin seeds.
4. When the cumin seeds crackle, add the green chillies, cinnamon, cloves, green cardamom, onions, ginger-garlic paste and sauté till the onions turn golden brown in colour.
5. Add the chilli powder, turmeric powder and tomato pulp and cook over a medium flame till the oil separates from the tomato gravy.
6. Add the dal mixture, ¾ cup of water and salt if required and simmer for 10 to 15 minutes.
7. Add the cream and mix well.
   Garnish with the coriander and butter and serve hot.

Handy tip : You will require 4 medium tomatoes to make 1½ cups of fresh tomato pulp.

～ Tittori (Parsi Dal) ～

•► Preparation time : 10 minutes. •► Cooking time : 40 minutes. •► Serves 6.

3 cups sprouted and peeled val dal (pavta)
1 cup chopped onions
1 tbsp ginger-garlic paste
½ tsp garam masala
½ tsp coriander (dhania) powder
½ tsp cumin (jeera) powder
½ tsp chilli powder
¼ tsp turmeric powder (haldi)
½ tsp sugar
1 cup finely chopped tomatoes
2 cups thick coconut milk, page 102
3 tbsp oil
salt to taste

1. Heat the oil in a large pan and add the onions and ginger-garlic paste to it.
2. When the onions turn translucent, add the garam masala, coriander powder,

cumin powder, chilli powder, turmeric powder, sugar, salt and tomatoes.
3. When the mixture leaves oil, add the val dal, and 2 cups of water and allow to cook on a low flame till the dal is done.
4. Add the coconut milk, mix gently and bring to a boil.
Serve hot.

~ Dal Moghlai ~

♦ Preparation time : 10 minutes. ♦ Cooking time : 25 minutes. ♦ Serves 4 to 6.

¾ cup toovar (arhar) dal
¼ cup chana dal (split Bengal gram)
1 cup chopped tomatoes
2 cups bottle gourd (doodhi / lauki), peeled and cut into big pieces
¼ tsp turmeric powder (haldi)
1 tsp cumin seeds (jeera)
½ tsp chopped garlic
1 tsp chopped green chillies
1 tsp grated ginger
¾ cup slices onions
2 tbsp oil
salt to taste

For the garnish
chopped coriander

1. Clean, wash and soak the dals for about 30 minutes. Drain.
2. Add the tomatoes, bottle gourd, turmeric powder, salt and 3 cups of water and pressure cook till the dals are tender.
3. Heat oil in a large pan and add the cumin seeds.
4. When the seeds crackle, add the garlic, green chillies, ginger and onions and sauté till the onions turn golden brown in colour.
5. Add the cooked dal mixture and 1 cup of water and bring to a boil.
   Serve hot garnished with the chopped coriander.

~ Panchmel Dal ~

1/3 cup chana dal (split Bengal gram)
1/3 cup toovar (arhar) dal
1/3 cup green moong dal (split green gram)
1 tbsp urad dal (split black lentils)
1 tbsp whole moong (whole green gram)
3 tsp chilli powder
1/4 tsp turmeric powder (haldi)
1 tsp coriander (dhania) powder
1/2 tsp garam masala
3 cloves (laung)
2 bay leaves (tejpatta)
1 tsp cumin seeds (jeera)
2 green chillies, slit
a pinch asafoetida (hing)
2 tsp amchur (dry mango powder)
2 tsp tamarind (imli) pulp

3 tbsp ghee
salt to taste

1. Clean and wash the dals and add 4 cups of water. Pressure cook for 2 to 3 whistles or till the dals are cooked.
2. In a bowl, combine the chilli powder, turmeric powder, coriander powder, garam masala with 3 tbsp of water and mix well to make the masala. Keep aside.
3. Heat the ghee in a pan and add the cloves, bay leaves, cumin seeds, green chillies and asafoetida. When the cumin seeds crackle, add the prepared masala paste and sauté for 1 to 2 minutes.
4. Add the cooked dal, amchur, tamarind pulp and salt and simmer for 5 to 7 minutes. Adjust the consistency of the dal before serving and if required, add some water.

～ **Dhabey Ki Dal** ～

Picture on facing page

•◦ Preparation time : 15 minutes. •◦ Cooking time : 30 minutes. •◦ Serves 4 to 6.

½ cup urad dal (split black lentils), with skin
¼ cup chana dal (split Bengal gram)
¼ cup rajma (kidney beans)
1 tbsp finely chopped garlic
1 cup finely chopped onions
2 green chillies, slit into 2
1 cup finely chopped tomatoes
1 tsp chilli powder
2 tsp cumin (jeera) powder
¼ cup chopped coriander leaves
1 tbsp kasuri methi (dry fenugreek leaves)
2 tsp oil
salt to taste

DHABEY KI DAL : Recipe above →

1. Clean, wash and soak the urad dal, chana dal and rajma in sufficient water for at least 6 hours.
2. Drain the soaked dals and rajma, add 6 cups water and pressure cook for 15 to 20 minutes or until the dals are completely cooked.
3. Heat the oil in a non-stick pan, add the garlic, onions and green chillies and sauté for 4 to 5 minutes till the onions are golden brown in colour.
4. Add the tomatoes, chilli powder, cumin powder and salt and cook over a high flame for 3 to 4 minutes.
5. Add the cooked dals and coriander, mix well and simmer for 5 to 7 minutes.
6. Add the kasuri methi, mix well and serve hot.

~ Khandeshi Dal ~

➤ Preparation time : 10 minutes. ➤ Cooking time : 25 minutes. ➤ Serves 8 to 10.

¾ cup urad dal (split black lentils)
¼ cup masoor dal (split red lentils)
¼ cup chana dal (split Bengal gram)
¼ cup toovar (arhar) dal
¼ cup green moong dal (split green gram)
¼ tsp turmeric powder (haldi)
salt to taste

For the masala powder
4 whole dry red chilies
½ cup sliced onions
¼ cup grated dry coconut (kopra)
2 tbsp coriander (dhania) powder
1 tsp whole peppercorns
4 to 5 cloves (laung)
25 mm. (1″) cinnamon (dalchini)

4 to 5 cardamom (elaichi)
4 to 5 cloves garlic

For the tempering
1 tsp mustard seeds (rai)
1 whole dry red chilli
1 bay leaf (tejpatta)
2 tbsp oil

For the masala powder
Dry roast all the ingredients on a tava.
Cool and blend in a mixer. Keep aside.

How to proceed
1. Clean, wash and soak the dals in water for about 30 minutes. Drain.
2. Add the turmeric powder, salt and 3 cups of water and pressure cook till the dals are tender.
3. Whisk the dal well, add 1 cup of water and the masala powder, mix and keep aside.
4. Heat the oil in another large pan and add the mustard seeds.
5. When the mustard seeds crackle, add the red chilli and bay leaf.

6. Add the cooked dal and bring to a boil.
7. Simmer for about 10 minutes on a low flame to enable all the flavours to blend well.
8. Garnish with the chopped coriander and serve hot preferably with bajra roti.

~ Shajahani Dal ~

1 cup chick peas (Kabuli chana), soaked overnight
1½ cups finely chopped onions
2 to 3 cloves (laung)
2 to 3 green cardamom (elaichi), crushed lightly
25 mm. (1") cinnamon (dalchini)
½ tsp chilli powder
½ tsp coriander (dhania) powder
½ tsp garam masala
2 tsp finely chopped green chilies
1 cup coconut milk, page 102
1 cup cream
2 tbsp ghee or oil
salt to taste

For the garnish
chopped coriander

1. Pressure cook the chick peas with salt 4 cups of water till they are overdone.
2. Blend the mixture to a smooth paste in a mixer. Keep aside.
3. Heat the ghee in a large pan and add the chopped onions.
4. Sauté till they are translucent and add the cloves, green cardamom, cinnamon and sauté for another minute.
5. Add the chilli powder, coriander powder, garam masala and green chillies and cook for another 30 seconds.
6. Add the puréed dal and salt and allow the mixture to come to a boil.
7. Add the coconut milk and cream and simmer till thick.
   Serve hot garnished with the chopped coriander.

~ Spicy Sindhi Dal ~

•• Preparation time : 10 minutes. •• Cooking time : 30 minutes. •• Serves 4 to 6.

1 cup chana dal (split Bengal gram)
1 cup finely chopped onions
1 tsp cumin seeds (jeera)
2 green chillies, slit
½ tsp turmeric powder (haldi)
½ cup finely chopped tomatoes
2 tbsp chopped coriander
1 tsp coriander-cumin seed (dhania-jeera) powder
½ tsp chilli powder
¼ tsp garam masala
2 tbsp ghee or oil
salt to taste

1. Clean, wash and soak the chana dal for 3 to 4 hours. Drain and keep aside.
2. Heat the ghee in a pan and fry the onions, cumin seeds and chillies until the onions are light brown in colour.

72

3. Add the chana dal, turmeric powder, salt and ½ cup of water. Cover and cook on a slow heat for 15 to 20 minutes until the dal is soft.
4. Add the tomatoes, coriander, coriander-cumin seed powder and chilli powder and cook for 1 minute. Sprinkle the garam masala on top.
   Serve hot.

～ Rangoon Na Vaal ～

Picture on facing page

↦ Preparation time : 10 minutes. ↦ Cooking time : 20 minutes. ↦ Serves 6 to 8.

2 cups Rangoon na vaal (broad field beans)
¼ tsp soda-bi-carb
¼ tsp ajwain carom seeds
¼ tsp asafoetida (hing)
½ tsp chilli powder
¼ tsp turmeric powder (haldi)
1 tbsp grated jaggery (gur)
1 tsp tamarind (imli) paste, optional
2 tbsp oil
salt to taste

1. Wash and soak the vaal overnight.
2. Drain the vaal, add the soda bi-carb and enough water to cover the vaal and pressure cook till done.

RANGOON NA VAAL : Recipe above ↦

3. Heat the oil, add the carom seeds, asafoetida, chilli powder, turmeric and stir for a few seconds.
4. Add the cooked vaal with 1 cup of water, jaggery, tamarind paste and salt and mix well.
5. Simmer for 5 to 7 minutes and serve hot.

Handy tip : If you do not wish to use jaggery and tamarind, use 3 cloves of crushed garlic at step 2.

Kottu (Sri Lankan Dal)

~ Preparation time : 10 minutes. ~ Cooking time : 20 minutes. ~ Serves 4.

¾ cup masoor dal (split red lentils)
1 teaspoon cumin seeds (jeera)
¼ teaspoon asafoetida (hing)
¼ teaspoon turmeric powder (haldi)
2 teaspoons chilli powder
¾ cup coconut milk, page 102
juice of ½ lemon
2 tablespoons oil
salt to taste

1. Clean, wash and soak the masoor dal in water for about 30 minutes. Drain.
2. Pressure cook the dal with turmeric powder, salt and 2½ cups of water till done.
3. Whisk well till the dal is mashed and keep aside.
4. Heat the oil in a large pan and add the cumin seeds. When the seeds crackle, add the asafoetida and chilli powder and sauté for a few seconds.
5. Add the cooked dal and bring to a boil.

6. Add the coconut milk and salt and ½ cup of water and simmer for 2 to 3 minutes.
7. Remove from the fire and add the lemon juice.
8. Mix well and serve hot.

Dals That Make A Meal

～ Dakho (Khati Mithi Dal With Vegetables) ～

↔ Preparation time : 25 minutes. ↔ Cooking time : 30 minutes. ↔ Serves 6.

For the dal and vegetable mixture
½ cup toovar (arhar) dal
2 tbsp chana dal (split Bengal gram)
¼ cup peeled and cubed red pumpkin (kaddu)
1 tbsp chopped brinjal (baingan), cut into 25 mm. (1″) pieces
½ cup peeled and cubed potatoes
½ cup finely chopped colocasia (patrel) leaves
¼ tsp turmeric powder (haldi)
salt to taste

For the tamarind-jaggery water
1 tbsp jaggery (gur)
1 tbsp tamarind (imlli)

For the tempering
2 tsp mustard seeds (rai)
2 cloves (laung)

2 sticks cinnamon (dalchini)
1 whole red chillies, broken into pieces
½ tsp chilli powder
¼ tsp asafoetida (hing)
3 tbsp oil

For the garnish
1 tbsp chopped coriander

1. Clean, wash and soak the dals in water for about 30 minutes. Drain.
2. Add turmeric power, salt and 1½ cups of water. Pressure cook till the dal is done.
3. Whisk well to mash the dal. Keep aside.
4. Boil the vegetables and colocasia leaves in water till done.
5. Drain and add to the mashed dal. Whisk again so some of the vegetables get mashed.
6. For the tamarind-jaggery water, wash the tamarind, add the jaggery and ¼ cup of water and boil till the tamarind is soft. Pass this mixture through a sieve and keep aside.
7. Heat the oil in a large pan and fry the mustard seeds, cloves, cinnamon, red chillies and chilli powder for a few seconds.
8. When the mustard seeds crackle, add the asafoetida and the dal and vegetable mixture.
9. Add the tamarind-jaggery water, turmeric powder and salt. Bring to a boil and simmer for about 5 minutes. Serve hot garnished with the chopped coriander.

∽ One Dish Dal ∽

↦ Preparation time : 20 minutes. ↦ Cooking time : 40 minutes. ↦ Serves 4.

2 tbsp yellow moong dal (split yellow gram)
¼ cup masoor dal (split red lentils)
1 green chilli
1 tsp grated ginger
1 tsp grated garlic
½ tsp turmeric powder (haldi)
6 to 8 bhindi (okra), cut into 25 mm. (1") pieces
½ cup cluster beans (guvar), cut into 25 mm. (1") pieces
½ cup peeled and cubed carrots
1 sweet corncob, cut into discs
1 cup peeled and cubed potatoes
2 brinjals, cut into 25 mm. (1") pieces
½ tsp cumin seeds (jeera)
6 to 8 curry leaves
½ tsp fenugreek (methi) seeds
¼ tsp asafoetida (hing)

1 tsp chilli powder
2 tbsp oil
salt to taste

1. Clean, wash and soak the dals for about 30 minutes. Drain.
2. Pressure cook with green chilli, ginger, garlic, turmeric powder, salt with 1 cup of water, till the dals are tender.
3. Whisk the dal till mashed, remove the green chilli and keep aside.
4. Heat the oil in a large pan and add the cumin seeds, curry leaves, fenugreek seeds and asafoetida and stir for a few seconds.
5. Add the bhindi, cluster beans, carrots, sweet corn, potatoes, brinjal and chilli powder and sauté for 5 to 7 minutes till the vegetables soften.
6. Add the cooked dal and 1 cup of water and salt and simmer for 5 to 10 minutes. Serve hot.

~ Dal Pinni ~

Picture on facing page

•• Preparation time : 10 minutes. •• Cooking time : 25 minutes. •• Serves 4 to 6.

2 tbsp yellow moong dal (split yellow gram)
2 tbsp chana dal (split Bengal gram)
2 tbsp masoor dal (split red lentils)
¼ cup chick peas (kabuli chana)
3 cups finely chopped spinach leaves (palak)
½ cup chopped cabbage
1 tbsp ginger-green chilli paste
¼ tsp turmeric powder (haldi)
½ cup chopped tomato
2 tbsp lemon juice
1 tsp sugar
2 tbsps oil
salt to taste

To be ground into a smooth paste
3 whole dry red chillies, broken

DAL PINNI : Recipe above →

1 tsp coriander seeds (dhania)
2 to 3 cloves (laung)
1 tsp poppy seeds (khus khus)
2 tbsp finely grated coconut
2 tbsp broken cashewnuts

How to proceed

1. Clean, wash and soak the dals and chick peas for about 2 hours. Drain.
2. Pressure cook with 3½ cups of water, turmeric powder, tomatoes, ginger-green chilli paste and salt till done.
3. Heat oil, add the spinach leaves and cabbage and sauté for about 5 minutes.
4. Add the cooked dal, sugar, masala paste and ½ cup of water and bring to a boil.
5. Simmer for 10 minutes on a low flame
6. Add the lemon juice and serve hot.

~ Chana Ghassi ~

↦ Preparation time : 20 minutes. ↦ Cooking time : 15 minutes. ↦ Serves 4.

1 cup kala chana (black horse gram), soaked overnight and boiled and drained
½ cup freshly grated coconut
25 mm. (1") stick cinnamon (dalchini)
4 cloves (laung)
3 peppercorns
3 whole dry red chillies, broken into pieces
½ cup sliced onions
salt to taste

1. Mix all the ingredients together, except the kala chana and dry roast on a tava until golden brown in colour. Allow it to cool.
2. Grind the mixture to a smooth paste with ½ cup of water.
3. Transfer to a pan, add 2 cups of water and salt and allow it come to a boil.
4. Add the boiled kala chana and allow it to simmer for a few minutes.
   Serve hot with steamed rice.

Handy tip : ½ cup of raw kala chana, when soaked and boiled will yield approx.
1 cup of boiled kala chana.

∼ **Panchras Dal** ∼

↔ Preparation time : 10 minutes. ↔ Cooking time : 40 minutes. ↔ Serves 4.

1 cup toovar (arhar) dal
1 raw banana, peeled and cut into big pieces
2 small brinjals (baingan), cut into big pieces
1 small potato, peeled and cut into big pieces
½ cup carrots, peeled and cut into big pieces
½ cup red pumpkin (kaddu), peeled and cut into big pieces
½ tsp turmeric powder (haldi)
½ tsp cumin seeds (jeera)
1 tsp coriander-cumin seeds (dhania-jeera) powder
½ tsp garam masala
2 tbsp oil
salt to taste

For the masala paste
½ tsp cumin seeds (jeera)
½ tsp coriander (dhania) seeds

1 whole dry red chili, broken int pieces
¼ cup grated dry coconut (kopra)
¼ cup chopped onions
1 tsp ginger-green chilli paste
½ tsp tamarind (imli)
1 tbsp oil

For the masala paste
1. Heat the oil in a pan and add the cumin and coriander seeds.
2. When the seeds crackle, add the dry red chilli, dry coconut and onions and cook stirring continuously till the mixture becomes golden brown.
3. Remove form fire, add the ginger-green chilli paste and tamarind and blend to a smooth paste. Keep aside.

How to proceed
1. Clean, wash and soak the toovar dal for about 30 minutes. Drain.
2. Add the salt, turmeric powder and 3 cups of water and pressure cook till the dal is done.
3. Whisk well till the dal is mashed.
4. Heat oil in a large pan and add the cumin seeds.
5. When the seeds crackle add the raw banana, brinjals, potato, carrots, red pumpkin.

coriander-cumin seed powder and garam masala and stir for some time.

6. Add 1 cup of water and salt, cover and cook till the vegetables are tender.
7. Add the cooked dal, masala paste and ½ cup of water.
8. Simmer on a low flame for about 10 minutes bring to a boil.
   Serve hot.

～ Dal Dhokli ～

•→ Preparation time : 20 minutes. •→ Cooking time : 1 hour. •→ Serves 6.

For the dal
2 cups toovar (arhar) dal
2 tbsp peanuts
8 pieces cocum, soaked
½ cup chopped tomatoes
3 to 4 tsp jaggery (gur)
½ tsp turmeric powder (haldi)
juice of ½ lemon
4 green chillies, slit
½ tsp chilli powder
1 tsp grated ginger
salt to taste

For the dhoklis
1 cup whole wheat flour (gehun ka atta)
½ tsp turmeric powder (haldi)

½ tsp chilli powder
½ tsp asafoetida (hing)
2 tbsp oil
¼ tsp carom seeds (ajwain)
salt to taste

For the tempering (of the dal)
¼ tsp mustard seeds (rai)
¼ tsp cumin seeds (jeera)
¼ tsp fenugreek (methi) seeds
10 curry leaves
2 cloves (laung)
2 sticks cinnamon (dalchini)
1 bay leaf (tejpatta)
2 small round red chillies
¼ tsp asafoetida (hing)
2 tbsp ghee
1 tbsp oil

Other ingredients
4 tbsp chopped coriander
2 bananas, peeled and chopped (optional)

For the dal
1. Wash and pressure cook the dal in 4 cups of water.
2. In another vessel, pressure cook the peanuts.
3. When the dal is cooked, cool slightly and blend till it is smooth.
4. Heat the ghee and oil in a large pan, add the mustard seeds, cumin seeds, fenugreek seeds, curry leaves, cloves, cinnamon, bay leaf, small round chillies and asafoetida and stir for 30 seconds.
5. Add 3 cups of water, cocum, tomato, jaggery, turmeric powder, lemon juice, green chillies, chilli powder and the ginger and simmer for 10 minutes.
6. Add the dal, peanuts and salt and simmer for 10 minutes. Keep aside.

For the dhoklis
1. Knead all the ingredients together with enough water to make a firm dough.
2. Divide into four portions and roll out into thin chapatis.
3. Gently roast on both sides and cool.
4. Cut the chapatis into diamonds or squares and keep asides.

How to proceed
1. Just before serving, boil the dal and slowly add in the dhokli pieces and the bananas and simmer for 15 minutes.
2. Garnish with the coriander and serve hot.

Handy tips : 1. Add the dhoklis one by one into the dal while stirring continuously as otherwise they could form one big lump.
2. Add more water if the dal thickens while simmering.

～ Dhansaak Dal ～

•• Preparation time : 25 minutes. •• Cooking time : 30 minutes. •• Serves 4.

½ cup toovar (arhar) dal
2 tsp yellow moong dal (split yellow gram)
2 tsp masoor dal (split red lentils)
2 tsp urad dal (split black lentils)
2 tsp val dal (split field beans)
¼ cup peeled and chopped potatoes
¼ cup chopped brinjal (baingan)
¼ cup peeled and chopped bottle gourd (doodhi / lauki)
¼ cup peeled and chopped red pumpkin (kaddu)
1 spring onion (including greens), chopped
1 tbsp chopped fenugreek (methi) leaves
½ cup chopped tomatoes
3 tsp tamarind (imli), soaked in ¼ cup of water
2 tbsp oil
salt to taste

To be ground into a paste
1 green chilli
3 whole red chillies
4 large cloves garlic
1 stick cinnamon (dalchini)
4 cloves (laung)
25 mm. (1") piece ginger
1 cardamom (elaichi)
1 tsp coriander (dhania) seeds
4 peppercorns
½ tsp cumin seeds (jeera)
2 tsp chopped coriander
2 tbsp water

To be made into a dry powdered masala
1 cardamom (elaichi)
1 stick cinnamon (dalchini)
1 clove (laung)

1. Clean and wash the dals.
2. Combine the dals and vegetables with 3 cups of water and and pressure cook for 3

whistles.
3. Liquidise the cooked dals and vegetables in a blender. Keep aside.
4. Heat the oil in a pan, add the prepared paste and sauté for 2 minutes.
5. Add the dals and vegetable purée, the dry powder masala, tamarind water and salt and boil for 10 to 15 minutes.
   Serve hot.

~ Darbari Dal ~

↔ Preparation time : 20 minutes. ↔ Cooking time : 30 minutes. ↔ Serves 6.

½ cup rajma (kidney beans), soaked overnight, cooked and drained
½ cup toovar dal (arhar)
½ cup masoor dal (split red lentils)
½ tsp turmeric powder (haldi)
1 cup bottle gourd (doodhi / lauki), cut into big pieces
½ cup red pumpkin (kaddu), cut into big pieces
½ cup babycorn, cut into big pieces
2 green chillies, slit
½ cup finely chopped onions
1 cup finely chopped tomatoes
2 tsp ginger-garlic paste
2 tbsp freshly grated coconut
2 tsp coriander-cumin seed (dhania-jeera) powder
1 tsp red chilli powder
1 tsp garam masala
3 tbsp oil

½ cup chopped coriander

1. Clean, wash and soak the dals for about 30 minutes. Drain.
2. Pressure cook the dals with 3 cups of water, turmeric powder and salt till done.
3. Whisk well till the dal is mashed and keep aside.
4. Heal oil in a large pan, add the onions and sauté till the onions turn translucent.
5. Add the tomatoes ginger-garlic paste, grated coconut, coriander-cumin seed powder, red chilli powder, garam masala and sauté for 2 to 3 minutes.
6. Add the pumpkins, baby corn, green chillies, cooked dal and 1 cup of water and bring to a boil.
7. Simmer till the vegetables are done and then add the coriander.
8. Simmer for a couple of more minutes and serve hot.

～ **Rajma Saagwala** ～

•• Preparation time : 15 minutes. •• Cooking time : 20 minutes. •• Serves 4.

½ cup rajma (kidney beans), soaked overnight, cooked and drained
3 cups chopped amaranth leaves (chawli)
½ tsp cumin seeds (jeera)
2 to 3 chopped green chillies
1 tsp chopped ginger
1 tsp chopped garlic
½ cup chopped onions
¼ tsp turmeric powder (haldi)
¼ cup cream
¼ tsp sugar (optional)
1½ tsp oil
salt to taste

1. Heat the oil and add the cumin seeds. When they crackle, add the green chillies, ginger, garlic and onions and sauté for 4 to 5 minutes.

2. Add the amaranth leaves, rajma, turmeric powder, salt and 1½ cups of water and bring to a boil.
3. Add the cream and sugar and simmer for another 5 to 7 minutes.
   Serve hot.

Basic Recipe

～ **Coconut Milk** ～

↔ Preparation time : 10 minutes. ↔ No Cooking. ↔ Makes 2½ to 3 cups.

1 fresh coconut, grated
2 cups warm water

1. To the grated coconut, add 2 cups of warm water.
2. Allow it to stand for 2 hours and then blend in a liquidizer for a couple of minutes.
3. Strain using a muslin cloth.
4. The strained liquid is thick coconut milk.
5. Repeat steps 2-3 for thin coconut milk.

Handy tip : Carefully grate only the white part of the coconut avoiding the brown
skin as it will change the colour of the cream.

A magazine by **TARLA DALAL**

FARAAL FOODS : **FEASTING WHILE FASTING**
LOOK & COOK *Modaks*
Picture-Perfect Bulletin Board
30-MINUTE MEALS

Book your copy now...

Price : Rs. 50/-

 Available at your nearest bookstore, newspaper stands and tarladalal.com

SUBSCRIBE NOW & Get Free
Bonus Membership at tarladalal.com

Pick any one of the subscription offers and send us a cheque or a Demand Draft in favour of "Sanjay & Co." along with your detailed address including pin code, telephone no. and e-mail address.

Addressed to :
Sanjay & Co. 353, A-1, Shah & Nahar Industrial Estate, Dhanraj Mill Compound, Lower Parel (W), Mumbai 400013. INDIA

5 years (30 issues) + 1 Year Free Membership = Rs. 1450/-[*]

3 Years (18 issues) + 9 Months Free Membership = Rs. 1080/-[*]

1 Year (6 issues) + 2 Months Free Membership = Rs. 340/-[*]

*Offer valid for shipments only within India and is inclusive of shipping & handling charges.

For overseas shipments log on to tarladalal.com

For more information, call us on our helpline no. (022) 2496 8068 on all weekdays between 9.30 a.m. and 4.30 p.m. or write to us at subscription@tarladalal.com

Best sellers on INDIAN COOKING
by *Tarla Dalal*

Desi Khana

Swadisht Subzian

Microwave Desi Khana

A New World of Idlis & Dosas

Paneer

Parathas

Chawal